Success with Shrubs and Trees in Containers

ALMUTH SCHOLZ

Series Editor
LESLEY YOUNG

Introduction

Contents

Balconies and patios can become pocket-sized gardens, particularly in urban and built up areas. Permanent plantings of container shrubs and trees in attractive containers will provide decorative features all year round. Evergreen foliage, colourful flowers and interesting fruits are not merely a visual delight for human eyes but also provide insects and birds with shelter and food.

This guide will introduce you to several of the most attractive container shrubs and trees, including many rarities. Excellent photographs demonstrate the wide range of colours and shapes that is available and author Almuth Scholz offers the reader a most practical selection of species and advice on suitable containers for planting them in. In the design section you will find examples of creative and imaginative plantings. Detailed illustrations provide step by step instructions on both planting and care, which will be easily followed even by the complete beginner. In addition you will also find useful, factual information on care, propagating and plant protection.

A balcony box with an attractive planting.

Lavender provides both scent and colour.

A butterfly on buddleia blossom.

The author
Almuth Scholz works in the gardening trade and has taught courses in garden design for many years. She owns a large garden with a patio where she has tried out many of the planting examples shown in this volume.

The photographer
Friedrich Strauss is a qualified landscape gardener and designer. His formal training in garden design was further supplemented by a course of studies in art history. He has published photographs in specialist gardening periodicals and other works for many years. Other photographs were supplied by well-known plant photographers (see acknowledgements on p. 61).

The illustrator
Marlene Gemke studied graphic design at the Fachhochschule Wiesbaden and is now self-employed as a scientific graphic artist. She has produced illustrations for several other titles in the "Success with ..." series.

NB: Please read the Author's notes on page 61 in order that your enjoyment of container shrubs and trees may remain unimpaired.

A patio garden

Container shrubs and trees look particularly attractive and decorative on balconies and patios where they provide interest throughout the year. The following pages supply information and advice on the right choice of plants and containers as well as practical tips on which compost to use.

Above: Catkins appear on the willow early in the year.
Left: Ornamental cherry, willow and tulips demonstrate the splendour of spring on this sunny balcony.

A patio garden

A pocket-sized garden

In an era when property prices continue to climb relentlessly, the dream of owning your own garden may seem almost impossible and balconies and patios are becoming increasingly important features for many people. Even in such a small space your ambition to create a tranquil corner of flowers and foliage can be fulfilled at a relatively reasonable cost. Compared with a conventional planting of pelargoniums or summer flowers, an arrangement of dwarf shrubs and trees offers extra possibilities for design. With only a few decorative plants, you will still be able to create a visually satisfying grouping. You may not achieve quite such a colourful display of flowers as you would with a balcony stocked with pelargoniums or petunias but the overall effect of such a planting should last all year round, which will more than compensate for the loss of temporary bright colour. Unlike many balcony plants, dwarf shrubs and trees do not restrict their display of beauty to a particular flowering period. Their foliage will change colour in the autumn and they often bear attractive fruits. A planting of dwarf shrubs and trees will also offer the following advantages.

● The plants will not have to be removed from their pots or taken in when autumn arrives.

● Many small creatures will take up permanent residence. Butterfly chrysalises or caterpillars wil be able to overwinter here. Beetles, ladybirds and useful lacewings will find shelter. Birds will find food in the form of fruit and berries. So, as you can see, you will not only be creating a peaceful spot in which to relax and recouperate yourself, you will also be offering a means of survival to a range of different species. Balconies and patios with varied plantings really do become true havens for everyone in an increasingly stressful environment.

Permanent planting

What does "permanent planting" mean? The usual balcony plants – like pelargoniums, petunias and lady's slipper – are not hardy. The very earliest that such plants can be planted out of doors is generally from the middle of the last month of spring, after all danger of frost is over. Later in the year, just before the first frosts arrive, about the middle of autumn, the wealth of flowers will be gone. Some plants, such as pelargoniums or even fuchsias, may be overwintered in frost-free rooms or propagated from cuttings. More often, however, these plants are considered as disposable and new ones are bought every year. This can

become an expensive business in the case of larger patios and balconies. The alternative is to install a permanent planting that will adorn your balcony or patio all year round. The lifespan of this kind of planting can range from several years to decades. Among the wide range of tough, hardy plants, many are suitable for mobile plant containers (see the tables on pp. 14 and 18). If you choose small-growing and slow-growing species, the time taken up by care will also be minimal. The initial purchase price may seem high but will soon be balanced out by these considerations.

The right position

Before deciding on plants for your patio or balcony, you should consider the following points.

● Check the light conditions in the position you intend to fill and choose suitable plants (see pp. 14 and 18). If suitable conditions are provided, these plants will reward you with visual pleasure even on gloomy autumn and winter days.

● A small balcony or loggia will provide room for only a few plants. Often, the only solution will be to fix flower boxes to the balcony railing. Even in a situation like this, however, you will still be able to experiment with dwarf shrubs and trees and try out various planting schemes.

Flowering shrubs and trees and bulbous plants create a tranquil atmosphere.

● Ground-floor flats or terraced houses offer further possibilities. You may be able to install plant containers in various sizes or a permanent group of capacious, extra-large containers. Try to design the progression from patio to garden proper as harmoniously as possible: the shrubs in the containers should complement the design of the garden.

● Even roof gardens may provide an opportunity to combine plants in large containers in an imaginative way. Sometimes, when you move to new premises, permanently fixed plant boxes or troughs may already be present. These are ideal for permanent plantings of dwarf shrubs and trees. All that is needed is a little creativity on your part and it is the aim of this guide to stimulate a desire in the reader to experiment and try out different ideas.

NB: If you are a tenant, you should discuss the installation of boxes or climbing frames, etc. with your landlord before you go ahead with such projects. If you live in a flat, you will also have to consider the weight-bearing properties of your balcony (see p. 11).

Botany and shapes of growth

The basic plants for any permanent planting are hardy, deciduous or coniferous dwarf shrubs and trees. Dwarf shrubs and trees are particularly small and also extremely slow-growing woody plants that will not attain their full size for many years. Many dwarf shrubs and trees are mountain plants or species from hot, dry steppes. Their unusual shapes of growth have evolved through adaptation to specific climatic conditions, for example, intense sunlight, exposure to excess wind or a lack of water and nutrients.

Even forest plants, however, for example, species that grow under large trees, are forced into dwarf growth by the pressures of competition. Obviously, the very varied origins of these plants means that their requirements with regard to position will also differ greatly. Of course, gardeners have also played a large part in the creation of the wide range of species found among dwarf plants. Special characteristics, such as an abundance of flowers, decoratively coloured leaves and fruit, are encouraged

and improved through crossing. A distinction can be made between deciduous and coniferous shrubs and trees and between summer green and evergreen plants.

Deciduous shrubs and trees
(illustration 1)

Shrubs and trees which shed their leaves do so in the autumn or winter, resulting in a wonderful array of autumnal colours. Evergreen types retain their foliage during the winter and often produce decorative, colourful leaves. In addition to the green foliage species, there are also some which display red or white variegated leaves

throughout the year. Even the shapes of the leaves can be very decorative. All deciduous woody plants bear attractive flowers in a large variety of colours and shapes with the exception of a few which have inconspicuous flowers. Bright fruits, unusually shaped branches and colourful bark are further attractive features of deciduous shrubs and trees, particularly in winter. When it comes to the variety of different shapes of growth, there is a definite distinction between small trees like the silver birch (*Betula pendula*), shrubs which spread like the hydrangea (*Hydrangea* hybrids) and upright-growing shrubs like *Ligustrum ovalifolium*.

1 Shapes of growth of deciduous trees: left tall, centre broad and bushy, right upright and bushy.

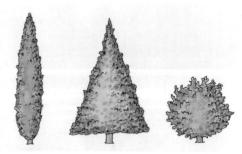

2 Shapes of growth of conifers: left a pillar, centre a cone shape, right a sphere.

Coniferous shrubs and trees

(illustration 2)

Depending on the species, conifers have soft, bristly, blunt or pointed needles. With the exception of the larch (*Larix kaempferi*), also previously known as *Larix leptolepis*, all dwarf conifers are evergreen. Their decorative value is determined by different coloured needles, such as yellow, light or dark blue, or blue green, as well as by the shapes of the needles and shapes of growth. Some species grow naturally in pillar shapes, such as *Taxus baccata* "Fastigiata". Others form regular cones, like *Thuja occidentalis* "Smaragd". Some even grow in a spherical shape, such as the dwarf species *Chamaecyparis pisifera* "Filifera Aurea Nana". In some conifers, such as the yellow *Juniperus chinensis* "Plumosa Aurea", the needles turn a copper colour during the winter.

Creeping and hanging woody plants

(illustration 3)

Among both the deciduous and the coniferous shrubs and trees, creeping or hanging forms can be found, such as ivy (*Hedera helix*) and the dwarf yew *Taxus baccata* "Repandens". These plants are good for closing gaps in permanent plantings and will droop artistically over the sides of containers. Some of the species that creep or hang, such as ivy (*Hedera helix*), will also climb.

Summer green or evergreen shrubs and trees

(illustration 4)

Summer green and evergreen species can be found among deciduous and coniferous plants. You will be able to watch the course of the seasons quite easily among the deciduous shrubs and trees. Before losing their leaves in the autumn, they will produce a

3 Shapes of growth: hanging and creeping.

mass of colourful foliage and fruit. They then display bare twigs and branches until the spring (see illustration 4, left). Evergreen plants, on the other hand, (see illustration 4, right), will fill your balcony with colour all year round. By contrast with the dwarf trees and shrubs, the above-ground parts of many woody perennials die off in late autumn (see illustration 4, centre). Dead twigs should be left until the spring and will look quite magical when covered with hoar frost or snow. In the spring, these woody perennials will produce shoots again from underground storage organs. There are also some evergreen and woody species among shrubs that are regarded as sub-shrubs, such as *Helianthemum* hybrids. Sub-shrubs, with their beautifully coloured flowers, make ideal companions for taller growing woody plants. Many scented plants and herbs are included among this group, such as lavender (*Lavendula officinalis*) and sage (*Salvia officinalis*).

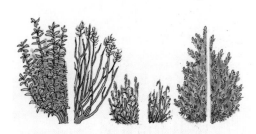

*4 **Various shapes:** deciduous or coniferous evergreen woody plants and shrubs.*

A patio garden

This balcony is splendid when the azalea is in flower.

Planning

A hardy, permanent planting on your balcony or patio is intended to give you much enjoyment for years on end and to manage on as little care as possible. With some good planning this should work well.

Requirements of plants: Careful selection is required. You will find advice on different requirements of various species in the tables on pages 14/15 and 18/19.

The preferences of the balcony owner: A permanent planting on a balcony or patio has a dual function, it should:

● create a pleasant atmosphere for the family and visitors;

● improve the overall visual impact of the house or building. Planning the positioning of the plant containers should be undertaken with these points in mind (see pp. 28/29).

The purposes of planning: Dwarf plants can be employed as spatial dividers as well as visual, sun, wind and noise screens.

Your legal respopnsibilities: As a tenant, you should always obtain permission from the owner of the building before undertaking any measures that will alter the general appearance of a balcony or patio. Large containers are usually a considerable weight and may cause damage. Find out before you begin what the weight-bearing properties of your balcony, roof garden or railings are. In general, additional weight (such as furniture and containers) on balconies of modern, well-constructed buildings should not exceed 250 kg (561 lb) per square metre, but you are strongly advised to consult a structural engineer or other qualified person on the subject of your own particular balcony.

Amount of care: You have a choice between easy-to-care-for, robust species or specialist plants requiring more attention (see pp. 20/21). Consider carefully how much time you have to devote to your plants and also think about when you go away on holiday.

Financial constraints: Dwarf plants are not exactly cheap, however, they do tend to live longer than other plants. Do ensure that you buy plants of good quality as many years of life in pots and containers will make high demands on the health and resistance of the plants. Buy young plants, as they are cheaper and more adaptable. A permanent planting need not all be accomplished during the first year. You can add to your collection with cheaper, annual summer plants (see p. 27).

Types of soil and compost

Different types of soil or compost are distinguished by the ratios of substances that they contain. If you wish your plants to thrive and live as long as possible, you will need to provide the right kind of growing medium for them. The main preconditions for good soil or compost include:
● air and water permeability;
● the ability to store water;
● a sufficient supply of nutrients;
● a stable structure;
● a stable pH value.
The pH value provides information on the acid content of soil or compost. Indicator sticks, which are obtainable from the gardening trade, can be used for measuring the pH values of soil. Two compost mixtures which fulfil the above requirements and can also be made up by people who do not own a garden, are given here.

Mixture 1: This mixture should have a pH value somewhere between 6.5 and 7. Mix one quarter of coarse sand and porous material, for example Hortag, with one quarter of bark humus, one quarter of ripe garden compost or compost from the gardening trade and a quarter of good garden or molehill soil. For those plants that like alkaline soil, add a handful of lime to every 10 litres (20 pt) of soil mixture. Plants with high nutrient

requirements.should also be supplied with a handful of controlled-release fertilizer (see fertilizing, pp. 48/49).

Mixture 2: This is particularly suited to plants that do not like alkaline soil and which require an acid compost with a pH value somewhere between 4 and 5. Make up the mixture in the same way as described above but substitute one quarter of peat for the ripe compost.

Ready-made composts: A number of ready-mixed composts can be obtained in the gardening trade. They generally contain a high proportion of peat and have been mixed with a lot of fertilizer. These kinds of compost are particularly unsuitable for large containers and boxes because although peat is able to store a high percentage of water, once it has dried out it does not easily absorb water again. Water then tends to run away in the gap between the wall of the container and the compost without the plant receiving any benefit.

NB: The natural world of peat bogs has become highly endangered by the extraction of peat for commercial purposes. Amateur gardeners should, therefore, only use peat and composts containing large amounts of peat in exceptional cases; for example, for rhododendrons. Bark humus and ripe garden compost are far more suitable for soil improvement.

Rhododendron flowers.

Deciduous shrubs and trees

There is a wide range of species of slow-growing deciduous shrubs and trees that are suitable for planting in large containers and boxes. Some of them produce an abundant show of flowers in the spring and then display coloured leaves and jewel-like fruits in the autumn. A number of evergreen varieties also bear multi-coloured foliage all year round.

An enchanting maple.

Cork-winged euonymus in autumn colours.

You may well have a hard time making choices among the deciduous shrubs and trees before you settle on the right plants for your patio. The great variety of unusual or bizarre shapes of leaf alone will be fascinating. Shapes of growth also vary. Growth may be tree-like, bushy or cushion-shaped. Numerous species grow in a creeping fashion, while others climb. Such plants provide interesting features on a balcony or patio.

Glowing yellow broom flowers.

Hydrangea in delicate pink.

Mahonia berries with a delicate bloom.

A patio garden

Deciduous shrubs and trees with restrained growth

Name	Position	Compost	Shapes of growth / Height in cm/in	Flowering time/colour / Fruit time/colour	Comments
Berberis species / berberis	○–◐	M1 / dry	bushy / 50-150 cm (20-60 in)	LSP-ES, yellow / MS-MA, black, red	thorns, autumn colours / red, part *, attracts bees
Buddleia alternifolia / buddleia	○	M1 / La	bushy / to 300 cm (120 in)	LSP, purple	cut back, WP, / prop. from cuttings
Buxus sempervirens / box	○–◐	M1	bushy / to 120 cm (48 in)	flowers / inconspicuous	*, p, attracts bees, / prop. from cuttings
Calluna vulgaris / heather	○–◐	M2 / N-, HI	bushy / 15-20 cm (6- 8 in)	MS-MA, white, / pink, red	*, cut back, attracts bees
Caryopteris clandonensis / blue spiraea	○	M1 / La, dry	bushy / 80-100 cm (32-40 in)	MS-MA, blue / silvery foliage	scented, attracts bees, / p, WP, prop. from cuttings
Chaenomeles hybrids / quince	○	M1 / dry	bushy / 100-150 cm (40-60 in)	MSP-LSP, red / EA-EW, yellow	thorny, attracts bees, / edible fruit
Cornus canadensis / dogwood	◐–●	M2 / moist, HI	creeping / 15-20 cm (6-8 in)	ES-MS, white / EA-MA, red	*, white upper leaves, / prop. from rhizome
Corylus avellana "Contorta" / corkscrew hazel	○	M1 / N+, moist	bushy / 200-300 cm (80-120 in)	LW-ESP, yellow	attracts bees, interesting / branch shapes
Cotoneaster species / cotoneaster	○–◐	M1 / dry	creeping / 20-30 cm (8-12 in)	LSP-ES, white / LS-EW, red	part *, p, attracts bees / prop. from downhanging shoots
Cytisus species ☠ / broom	○–◐	M1 / La, N-, dry	creeping / 10-80 cm (4-32 in)	LSP-ES, yellow / purple	WP, attracts bees, / green bark
Daphne cneorum ☠ / garland flower	○–◐	M1 / La, dry	bushy / 20 cm (8 in)	MSP-LSP, pink	*, scented plant
Deutzia gracilis	○–◐	M1 / N+, La, moist	bushy / 100 cm (40 in)	LSP-MS, white	p, attracts bees
Erica species / heather	○–◐	mainly / M2	bushy / 15-20 cm (6-8 in)	LW-MSP/MS-MA / white, pink, red	M1 for snowy heather, / cut back
Euonymus alata ☠ / cork-winged spindle tree	○–◐	M1	bushy / 150 cm (60 in)	LSP-ES, white / EA-MA, orange-red	attracts bees, / red colour in autumn
Euonymus fortunei / spindle tree	◐–●	M1 / N+, dry	creeping / 30-150 cm (12-60 in)	inconspicuous / flowers	*, also varieties with / coloured leaves
Gaultheria procumbens / partridge berry	◐–●	M2 / HI	creeping / 20 cm (8 in)	MS-LS, pink / MA-EW, red	*, prop. from rhizomes
Genista lydia ☠ / broom	○	M1 / La, N-	bushy / 60 cm (24 in)	LSP-ES, yellow	green bark
Hedera helix ☠ / ivy	◐–●	M1 / La, dry	climbing / 20-300 cm (8-120 in)	takes at least five / years to flower	*, also varieties with / several colours
Hydrangea macrophylla / hydrangea	◐	M1 / N+, moist	bushy / 100 cm (40 in)	ES-MS, pink, / red, blue	prop. from rhizomes
Hypericum species / St John's wort	○–◐	M1	bushy / 15-80 cm (6-32 in)	LSP-MA, yellow	cut back, WP, attracts / bees
Ilex crenata ☠ / holly	○–◐	M1	bushy / 50-200 cm (20-80 in)	LSP, white / EA-EW, red	*, dioecian, also / white variegated forms
Jasminum nudiflorum / winter jasmine	◐	M1	hanging / 200-300 cm (80-120 in)	LW-MSP, yellow	green bark, prop. from / rhizomes
Kalmia angustifolia "Rubra" ☠ / sheep laurel	◐–●	M2 / HI, N-, moist	bushy / 100 cm (40 in)	ES-MS, red	one of the most beautiful / * deciduous trees

Deciduous shrubs and trees with restrained growth

Name	Position	Compost	Shapes of growth Height in cm/in	Flowering time/Colour Fruit time/colour	Comments
Lespedeza thunbergii weeping bush clover	○ – ◑	M1 dry	bushy 150 cm (60 in)	MS-MA, pink	prop. from rhizomes, WP
Leucothoe walteri	◑ – ●	M2 HI, moist	bushy 150 cm (60 in)	MSP-LSP, white	*, purple red in winter
Ligustrum vulgare ☠ privet	◑ – ●	M1	bushy 200 cm (80 in)	ES-MS, white MA-EW, black	attracts bees, prop. from rhizomes
Mahonia aquifolium Oregon grape	◑ – ●	M1 moist	bushy 100 cm (40 in)	ESP-MSP, yellow MS-EA, black	*, reddish in winter, attracts bees
Perovskia species Russian sage	○	M1 N-, La, dry	bushy 80 cm (32 in)	MS-MA, blue	silvery foliage, scented plant, cut back, WP
Potentilla fruticosa shrubby cinquefoil	○	M1 dry	bushy 30-80 cm (12-32 in)	LSP-MA, yellow	attract bees, p
Prunus cistena copper-leaved ornamental plum	○	M1 N+	bushy 200 cm (80 in)	LSP, white	red foliage, shoots red
Prunus tenella ornamental almond	○	M1 La	bushy 50-150 cm (20-60 in)	MSP-LSP, pink	copes well with dryness
Prunus triloba ornamental almond	○ – ◑	M1 La	bushy 200 cm (80 in)	MSP-LSP, pink	abundant flowering, also as small standard
Pyracantha species firethorn	◑ – ●	M1 dry	bushy 250 cm (100 in)	LSP-ES, white EA-EW, orange	attracts bees, *, deep rooted
Rhododendron species rhododendron	◑ – ●	M2 HI, moist	bushy 50-150 cm (20-60 in)	MSP-ES, lilac, red, pink, white	*, attracts bees, remove dead flowers
Rhus typhina "Dissecta" sumach	○ – ◑	M1	tree-like 300 cm (120 in)	ES-MS, green LS-ESP, red	red autumn colour, decorative foliage
Rosa species rose	○	M1 N+	bushy 50 cm (20 in)	ES-MA, many colours	cut back
Salix caprea "Pendula" willow	○ – ◑	M1 moist	small stems 150-200 cm (60-80 in)	ESP-MSP, catkins	attracts bees, cut back
Salix hastata "Wehrhahnii" willow	○	M2 moist, HI	bushy 30-100 cm (12-40 in)	ESP-MSP, catkins	attracts bees, very decorative
Skimmia species skimmia	◑ – ●	M2 HI, N+	bushy 50 cm (20 in)	MSP-LSP, white MA-EW, red	*, scented, protect from winter sunlight
Spiraea species spiraea	○ – ◑	M1	bushy 30-80 cm (12-32 in)	MS-MA, red, pink, white	attracts bees, p
Stephanandra tanakae stephanandra	○ – ◑	M1 dry	bushy 50 cm (20 in)	LSP-ES, yellowish	attracts bees, p, yellow autumn colour
Symphoricarpos species ☠ snowberry	◑ – ●	M1	bushy 50-200 cm (20-80 in)	ES-MS, pink MS-EW, red, white	some species *, attracts bees
Vaccinium vitis-idaea cranberry	◑	M2 HI, N-	bushy 30 cm (12 in)	LSP-ES, white EA-EW, red	*, attracts bees, edible fruit
Viburnum davidii ☠ viburnum	◑ – ●	M1 moist	bushy 100 cm (40 in)	ES, pink-white LS, dark blue	WP, high value as decoration
Viburnum opulus "Nanum" ☠ common snowball	◑ – ●	M1 moist	spherical 60 cm (24 in)	ESP-MSP, pink, white	shoots orange red, also * species, partly scented
Weigela florida "Purpurea" weigela	○ – ◑	M1 dry	bushy 50-150 cm (20-60 in)	ES-MS/MA, red, pink	red foliage, attracts bees, p, prop. from cuttings

○ = sun, ◑ = semi-shade, ● = shade, ☠ = toxic, p = copes with cutting, WP = winter protection, La = likes alkaline soil, HI = hates lime
M1 = mixture 1 (p. 11), M2 = mixture 2 (p. 11), N+ = nutrient rich, N- = nutrient poor, * = evergreen,
ESP = early spring; MSP = mid spring; LSP = late spring; S = summer; A = autumn; W = winter

Dwarf hemlock fir.

A host of suitable conifers

The range of dwarf conifers is also quite considerable. All are evergreen with the exception of the larch (*Larix kaempferi*). This species turns golden yellow in autumn before dropping its soft needles. Other conifers have larger, sharper needles which can be useful in that they will often protect you from unwanted "guests" on your balcony or patio.

Pendulous larch, fir and juniper.

Creeping juniper.

Delicate Sawara cypress.

Coniferous shrubs and trees provide an astonishing variety of possibilities. You will find species in the most varied shades of green that are wonderful for combining and matching. Some form delicate or lacy foliage and branches; others produce unusually shaped ones. The shoots in spring and the fruits in the autumn usually provide some interesting variation in colour. There are also weeping and creeping varieties.

Beautiful but toxic: yew berries.

Shoots of Pinus mugo.

A patio garden

Sub-shrubs

Name	Position	Compost	Shape of growth / Height in cm/in	Flowering time/Colour / Fruit time/Colour	Comments
Dryas octopetala	○	M1 dry	creeping 10 cm (4 in)	LSP-ES, white MS-MA, feathery	*, decorative seedheads
Helianthemum hybrids rock rose	○	M1 La, dry	bushy 15-20 cm (6-8 in)	ES-LS, yellow white, red	*, cut back
Hyssopus officinalis hyssop	○	M1 dry	bushy 50 cm (20 in)	ES-LS, blue	culinary herb, cut back
Iberis species candytuft	○	M1 dry	bushy 15-20 cm (6-8 in)	ESP-MSP, white MS-EA, blue	some species *, p
Lavandula angustifolia lavender	○	M1 La, dry	bushy 50-80 cm (20-32 in)	ES, inconspicuous	*, silvery foliage, attracts bees, scented
Pachysandra terminalis ☠ pachysandra	◑ – ●	M1 moist	creeping 20 cm (8 in)	ES-MS, blue	*, forms rhizomes
Salvia officinalis sage	○	M1 dry	bushy 50 cm (20 in)	ES-MS, yellow	scented, culinary herb, attracts bees, p, seed
Santolina chamaecyparissus cotton lavender	○	M1 dry	bushy 40-50 cm (16-20 in)	MS-MA, pink	silvery foliage, scented, *, WP, cut back, seed
Teucrium chamaedrys germander	○ – ◑	M1 La	bushy 20 cm (8 in)	ESP-MSP, blue	attracts bees, p
Vinca minor lesser periwinkle	◑ – ●	M1 moist	creeping 20 cm (8 in)		*, attracts bees

Conifers with restrained growth

Name	Position	Compost	Shapes of growth / Height in cm/in	Colour of needles	Comments
Abies balsamea "Nana" silver fir	○ – ◑	M1 moist	spherical 50-80 cm (20-32 in)	dark green	radially positioned needles, slow growing
Chamaecyparis lawsoniana "Ellwoodii" Lawson cypress	○ – ◑	M1 La	pillar shaped to 200 cm (80 in)	grey blue	slow growing
Chamaecyparis lawsoniana "Minima Glauca", Lawson cypress	○ ◑	M1 La	spherical 100 cm (40 in)	matt blue	also yellow colours, more cone-shaped in old age
Chamaecyparis obtusa "Nana Gracilis" Hinoki cypress	◑	M1 La	cone shaped 200 cm (80 in)	green	slow-growing, protect from winter sun
Chamaecyparis pisifera "Boulevard" Sawara cypress	○ – ◑	M1 La	cone shaped 150 cm (60 in)	steel blue	robust, very decorative
Chamaecyparis pisisfera "Filifera Aurea Nana" Sawara cypress	○ – ◑	M1 La	flat spherical 100-150 cm (40-60 in)	yellow green	very resistant to sunlight
Chamaecyparis pisifera "Filifera Nana" Sawara cypress	○ – ◑	M1 La	flat spherical 100 cm (40 in)	green	tips thread-like
Juniperus chinensis "Blaauw" Chinese juniper	○ – ◑	M1 dry	bushy 150-200 cm (60-80 in)	grey blue	one of the most beautiful bush junipers
Juniperus chinensis "Old Gold" Chinese juniper	○ – ◑	M1 dry	flattish 100 cm (40 in)	golden yellow	slow-growing
Juniperus chinensis "Plumosa Aurea" Chinese juniper	○ – ◑	M1 dry	bushy 100 cm (40 in)	golden yellow	bronze yellow in winter
Juniperus communis "Repanda" common juniper	○ – ◑	M1 dry	cushion-like 30 cm (12 in)	silvery green	may grow to 1.5 m (60 in) wide

Name	Position	Compost	Shapes of growth Height in cm/in	Colour of needles	Comments
Juniperus horizontalis "Glauca" creeping juniper	○ – ◐	M1 dry	mat-like 30 cm (12 in)	steel blue	the variety with the bluest needles, slow growing
Juniperus sabina "Tamariscifolia" savin	○	M1 La	bushy 100 cm (40 in)	fresh green	several metres wide in old age
Juniperus squamata "Blue Carpet" scaly-leaved Nepal juniper	○	M1 dry	flat 20-30 cm (8-12 in)	blue grey	may grow up to 2 m (80 in) wide
Juniperus squamata "Blue Star" scaly-leaved Nepal juniper	○	M1 dry	semi-spherical 70-80 cm (28-32 in)	blue grey	suitable for troughs
Microbiota decussata	◐ – ●	M1 dry	flattish habit 20 cm (8 in)	light green	copper brown in winter
Picea abies "Echiniformis" Norway spruce	○ – ◐	M1 N+	rounded 20-30 cm (8-12 in)	yellow green	very slow growing
Picea abies "Little Gem" Norway spruce	○ – ◐	M1 N+, moist	flatly spherical 40 cm (16 in)	light green	flattish depression in the centre
Picea abies "Nidiformis" Norway spruce	○ – ◐	M1 N+, moist	flat roundish 80-100 cm (32-40 in)	light green	flattish depression in the centre
Picea abies "Pygmaea" Norway spruce	○ – ◐	M1 N+, moist	cone shaped 100 cm (40 in)	fresh green	oldest known dwarf variety
Picea glauca "Conica" Canadian spruce	○ – ◐	M1 N+, moist	cone shaped 100-200 cm (40-80 in)	fresh green	requires position with high humidity
Picea glauca "Echiniformis" Canadian spruce	○ – ◐	M1 N+, moist	rounded 50 cm (20 in)	blue green	grows very slowly
Picea omorika "Gnom" Serbian spruce	○ – ◐	M1 La	cone shaped 150 cm (60 in)	green, white stoma lines	sensitive to waterlogging
Pinus mugo "Gnom" mountain pine	○	M1 dry, N-	spherical 200 cm (80 in)	deep green	very resiny buds
Pinus mugo "Mops" mountain pine	○	M1 dry, N-	spherical 150 cm (60 in)	dark green	often dome-shaped
Pinus mugo pumilio mountain pine	○	M1 dry, N-	low 200 cm (80 in)	dark green	branches are bent like knees
Pinus pumila "Glauca" dwarf Scots pine	○ – ●	M1 dry, N-	bushy 200 cm (80 in)	grey blue	red male flowers, slow growing
Pinus sylvestris "Watereri" Scots pine	○	M1	pillar shaped 200 cm (80 in)	blue grey	very robust, popular form
Taxus baccata "Fastigiata" ☠ Irish yew	◐ – ●	M1 La	pillar shaped 300 cm (120 in)	dark green	shaping cut possible, also yellow variety
Taxus baccata "Repandens" ☠ yew	○ – ●	M1 La	low 40-50 cm (16-20 in)	dark green	will become 2-3 m (80-120 in) wide
Taxus baccata "Nana" ☠ yew	○ – ◐	M1 La	low 100 cm (40 in)	matt green	will grow to 3 metres (120 in) wide
Thuja occidentalis "Danica" arbor-vitae	○ – ◐	M1	spherical 30-60 cm (12-24 in)	fresh green	beautiful round shape
Thuja occidentalis "Rheingold" arbor-vitae	○ – ◐	M1 moist	spherical 150 cm (60 in)	golden yellow	copper coloured in winter, slow growing
Tsuga canadensis "Jeddeloh" eastern hemlock	○ – ◐	M1 moist	semi-spherical 25 cm (10 in)	fresh green	flattish depression in the centre

○ = sun, ◐ = semi-shade, ● = shade, ☠ = toxic, p = copes with cutting, WP = winter protection, La = likes alkaline soil, Hl = hates lime
M1 = mixture 1 (p. 11), M2 = mixture 2 (p. 11), N+ = nutrient rich, N- = nutrient poor, * = evergreen,
ESP = early spring; MSP = mid spring; LSP = late spring, S = summer; A = autumn; W = winter

A patio garden

Popular plants for plant lovers

In addition to the species mentioned on the previous pages there are also many shrubs and trees which I usually refer to as popular specialist plants. These species cannot be obtained everywhere and both the prices and the amount of care required are somewhat greater. They will require even more attention if they are planted in large containers rather than in the ground and during the winter they should be placed in a sheltered position. Among this group, however, there are very many decorative and beautiful species. The following plants will provide interest even on the gloomiest winter's day and also in early spring.
● Beauty berry *(Callicarpa bodinieri)*: violet berries in mid autumn to early winter.
● Smoke tree *(Cotinus coggyria* "Royal Purple")*: feathery fruit stands in early autumn to early winter.
● Witch hazel *(Hamamelis japonica)*: yellow or red flowers in early to late winter.
● *Pieris japonica*: white, bell-shaped flowers in late winter to early spring, reddish shoots.
● *Corylopsis pauciflora*: yellow flowers in early to mid spring.
● Dwarf forsythia *(Forsythia ovata* "Minigold")*: yellow flowers in early to mid spring.

Mini trees: These trees grow very slowly if planted in containers and given a low dosage of nutrients. They will remain small for years on end. They are most attractive as solitary plants. The following are particularly suitable:
● Japanese maple *(Acer palmatum* "Dissectum")*: red autumn colouring, attractive foliage.
● Japanese maple *(Acer palmatum* "Dissectum Atropurpureum")*: red foliage and intense red autumn colouring.
● Nordic dwarf birch *(Betula nana)*: gnarled branches, blackish-grey bark, autumn colour orange yellow.
● silver birch *(Betula pendula* "Youngii")*: gnarled branches, picturesque growth.
● Indian bean tree *(Catalpa bignonioides* "Nana")*: great decorative value in leaves, flowers and fruit, attracts bees.
Two late-flowering species:
● dwarf lilac *(Syringa microphylla)*: lilac flowers in early summer and again in early to mid autumn.
● fuchsia *(Fuchsia magellanica)*: if given a protected position hardy, red flowers from mid summer to mid autumn. Usually dies back but will produce shoots again after pruning.
Decorative conifers:
● dwarf Weymouth pine *(Pinus strobus* "Nana")*.
● Japanese larch *(Larix kaempferi)*, which can also be

obtained with a more pendulous shape of growth.

Pure species of shrubs and trees

These are species which have not been "interfered with" by raisers. Among them are found many types with dwarf growth. As a rule, such plants growing wild would not survive digging up, transportation and replanting or will simply not thrive. It is in any case against the law to remove most wild plants from their natural habitat. If the plants are not entirely protected, however, you may be allowed to take some seed. With a little luck and green fingers you may succeed in propagating new plants from seed (see p. 54). Alternatively, you could seek either plants or seed in a good nursery. These plants will grow in flowerboxes and large containers without any problems. Particularly attractive species include:
● St John's wort *(Hypericum androsaemum)*
● broom *(Genista tinctoria)*
● broom *(Genista pilosa)*
● dwarf privet *(Ligustrum vulgare* "Lodense")*
● *Ononis spinosa*
● rose *(Rosa gallica)*
● rose *(Rosa villosa)*
● woolly willow *(Salix lanata)*
● dwarf viburnum *(Viburnum opulus* "Compactum")*.

Glowing fruits on the beauty berry.

St John's wort.

A thorny Ononis spinosa.   *Witch hazel.*

Dwarf mountain laurel.

Enchanting rarities

Specialist plants are conspicuous for their unique flowers and often bear unusual fruits. Many also display splendid autumn colouring. These rarities are usually only obtainable from specialised nurseries and will often require a lot of care. However, any extra effort on your part will be well rewarded by the unusual beauty of these plants.

Dwarf birch in autumn.

Containers

Decorative large containers and troughs will emphasize the beauty of dwarf shrubs and trees. In addition to visual impact and your own personal taste, however, you should consider the following points when choosing containers.

● Measurements: Large containers for dwarf shrubs and trees should have minimum dimensions of 25 x 25 x 25 cm (10 x 10 x 10 in). Flowerboxes should be at least 60 cm (24 in) long and as wide and deep as possible.

● Weight: Clay and stone containers planted with large shrubs or trees may be extremely heavy. Make sure that you obtain enough information beforehand on the weight-bearing capacity of your balcony or roof garden (see p. 10).

Large containers are also difficult to transport. Often, however, specialist firms will help you with this.

● Stability and firm standing: Shrubs and trees that grow tall require a heavy or well-secured container so that strong winds cannot cause them to tip over. The pressure exerted by the roots of some plants will also place great demands on the material the vessel is made of.

● Water drainage: The containers should prevent excess water from running down the façade of a building and becoming a nuisance to passersby or other tenants.

● Resistance to frost: Make sure before purchasing that the containers are frost-resistant. Terracotta pots are, unfortunately, often not completely frost-resistant.

Materials: You will find the greatest variety among containers for sale in specialist outlets.

● Plastic: Advantages include less weight; lower prices; shatter-proof; narrow temperature fluctuations within the vessel; low rate of evaporation. Disadvantages include not usually being very attractive; non-permeable to water and air.

● Moulded cement: Advantages include durability; harmless to plant organisms; cheap; many colours and shapes. Disadvantages include being heavy; sensitive to blows or knocks.

● Clay and terracotta: Advantages include being decorative; many colours and shapes; water- and air-permeable; do not tip over easily. Disadvantages include being heavy; high moisture evaporation rate through the vessel walls and, with this, a danger of drying out; unattractive salt marks from calcium and fertilizer residues; breakable.

● Wood: Advantages include being decorative; you can make them yourself; water- and air-permeable. Disadvantages include being very heavy; will require plant-friendly preservative treatment.

● Concrete and natural stone, do-it-yourself kits using U- and L-shaped stones: Advantages include being

1 A balcony box hung from a railing.

2 A wooden box screwed to a railing.

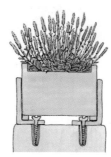

3 A box dowelled into masonry.

4 Wind security for pots with tall plants.

5 Containers shaped in quarter circles stand very firmly.

railing. Here, too, safety devices should be used to prevent anything from falling. The fixtures can be screwed straight into the wooden box.

Concrete boxes
(illustration 3)

Patios often have stone or brick edges. The fixtures for very heavy containers can be dowelled straight into the wall. Right-angled shelf irons are also suitable as fixtures.

Securing pots against wind
(illustration 4)

The wind will blow particularly strongly against single standing pots planted with trees. Here, a clay pot has been chained securely to the wall, ensuring that it will be safe even during a storm.

Quarter circle containers
(illustration 5)

This type of vessel can fit snugly into a corner of a balcony or patio. They

can be paired up and set right up against a wall or railing. They are very stable when lying on the ground and, as a rule, will not require any additional fixing. Four such pots, arranged in a circle, form an interesting ensemble but do require space.

Pot hangers
(illustration 6)

Pots standing on the floor of a balcony are a pleasure for the owner but do not work from a distance. You can put this right by standing the pot in a hanger that can be hooked on to a railing. These hangers are not expensive and can be obtained from specialist shops.

6 A hanger for pots on railings.

decorative; many variations; you can construct them yourself. Disadvantages include being very heavy and therefore hardly transportable.

Securing large containers

Containers holding plants should be secured well so that they are unable to tip over, even in storms and heavy rain. Use only non-rusting metal attachments to avoid ugly rust stains on walls.
NB: Remember that shrubs and pendulous

woody plants are very heavy.

Hanging balcony boxes
(illustration 1)

You can buy ready-made fixtures for balcony railings with balcony boxes to match. They should have "safety lips" to prevent the boxes from tipping up.

Wooden boxes
(illustration 2)

Containers made of wood can often be placed directly on the

Innovative design

With the information you have gathered from the previous pages you can now choose from the multitude of suitable dwarf shrubs and trees and put together a permanent planting according to your own preferences. Further inspiration may be gleaned from the next few pages.

Above: Hydrangea flowers in deep purple blue. Hydrangeas are also available in pink or white. Left: This early summer balcony contains a colourful display of flowers: laburnum, rhododendron, snowball, bleeding heart, thrift and campanula.

Using colour

When choosing your plants, you will be astonished by the wide range of colours of flowers and fruit, of leaves, needles and bark that is available. If you try to follow the colours found in nature, for example, on a flowering hillside or in a colourful, flowering hedgerow, you will never run short of ideas. On the other hand, to avoid your planting becoming too bright or overdone, you must plan your colour combinations very carefully.

Uniform colour: A planting purely in white (see right), yellow, blue or red can look very handsome.

Different shades of one colour: This means combining colours that blend into each other, such as yellow, orange and red (see p. 32) or red, violet and blue violet.

Complementary colours: Among these are yellow and lilac (see p. 27), blue and orange, as well as red and green. These pairings have the effect of making each other appear more glowing.

Colour trio: A combination of yellow, red and blue (see p. 7) looks very lively.

Colour effects: Colours also affect our moods.

● White transmits light and gives other colours more depth, thereby increasing their colour value.

● Yellow, the colour of the sun, transmits warmth, as do neighbouring shades of red and orange.

● Red has an enlivening effect.

● Blue, violet and green are thought to be cool.

Check the surroundings: Also consider the background when designing your planting. Light colours look very gentle against dark wood; intense colours work against a white housewall.

Spatial effects: Colours can visually alter spaces.

● Bright colours like yellow, orange and red will crowd into the foreground which will make a space seem smaller.

● Pastel shades, on the other hand, especially when mixed with silvery foliage, seem to expand a space.

In this way a small balcony can be made to gain depth and space.

Designs in one colour look extremely elegant.

Combining plants

Only place dwarf plants together if they have similar requirements with respect to light, temperature, soil and nutrient and water supplies.

Annual summer flowers may be used as companion plants for permanent plantings. These plants will, however, have a higher demand for nutrients than dwarf shrubs and trees and may compete with them. Good partners for one flowering season would include:

● For sunny positions, alyssum (*Alyssum maritimum*) in shades of white, pink or lilac, then blue-flowering lobelia (*Lobelia erinus*), yellow-flowering *Asteriscus maritimus* and *Verbena* hybrids with white, pink, red or violet flowers.

● For semi-shady positions *Brachycome iberidifolia* is very suitable with its white, blue or reddish-pink flowers and also busy Lizzies (*Impatiens* hybrids) in white, pink, red and violet. Shrubs, in particular the ground-covering, smaller species, are also suitable for combinations.

● For sunny balconies and patios you can use *Aubreta* hybrids, cushion phlox (*Phlox subulata* hybrids) in white, pink and lilac, stonecrop (*Sedum* species) in yellow and red, as well as *Campanula* species.

● Among shade-loving shrubs the following are recommended: *Viola cornuta* hybrids in shades of blue, yellow or white and variegated dead nettle (*Lamium maculatum*) with lilac purple flowers.

Climbing species: Among these are attractive varieties which can be used in both hanging and climbing forms.

Large container shrubs and trees that are non-hardy in a temperate climate may accompany the permanent planting during the warmer times of year (see p 34). They should be overwintered in frost-free conditions.

Complementary colours glow like jewels.

Skilful planting in large containers

When using dwarf shrubs and trees you will find that you have a large number of design options. The most important points to note are shown in the following examples. Planting techniques are described on page 46.

Compositions with depth
(illustration 1)

You should alternate plants of different heights in large boxes to obtain the effect of spatial depth. Creeping plants should always be placed around the edges where they can hang down artistically. This example is notable for the charming contrast of flower and leaf shapes as well as the different colours (see p. 26).
Container: A box with a length of 80 cm (32 in).
Position: Sunny.
Arrangement: Blue caryopteris (*Caryopteris clandonensis*) is flanked on the left by lavender (*Lavandula officinalis*) and on the right by cotton lavender (*Santolina chamaecyparissus*) (senstive to frost!) and sage (*Salvia officinalis*). Further to the right, growing over the edge,

2 The leading plant and underplanting complement each other. The different shapes of growth make the design more interesting.

is broom (*Genista tinctoria* "Plena"). This composition is further complemented by annual summer flowers (see p. 27).

A box with a "leader" plant
(illustration 2)

One "leader" plant dominates this whole box. Evergreen plants with various leaf and growth shapes make a charming combination.
Container: A box with a length of 60 cm (24 in).
Position: Sunny.
Arrangement: The "leader" plant is a Serbian spruce (*Picea omorika* "Nana") with cone-shaped growth. To the left is a creeping dwarf juniper (*Juniperus procumbens* "Nana"); in the foreground a dwarf

Cotoneaster dammeri "Streib's Findling". A splash of colour is provided by *Potentilla fruticosa* on the right.
My tip: For balcony boxes you should choose plants that are no taller than 80 cm (32 in).

A tranquil combination
(illustration 3)

If you choose only a few species with a similar height of growth, and restrict yourself to a few colours, your box will appear quiet and introspective. However, do not place the plants strictly symmetrically in the box as this will soon look boring. Instead, stagger them a little. This example will provide a

1 Great depth is obtained in this luxuriantly planted box.

display of flowers from winter to spring.
Container: A box with a length of 60 cm (24 in).
Position: Sunny.
Arrangement: Four plants of *Erica herbacea* and three plants of dwarf broom (*Cytisus decumbens*).

Large containers holding standards
(illustration 4)

Many deciduous shrubs and trees can be grown as standards (see pp. 36/37). Even on small balconies, there should still be enough space for a standard.
Container: A container with a diameter of 50 cm (20 in).
If you plan to move it around frequently, purchase one with carrying handles or

3 *This composition is effective in its discreet colours and shapes.*

obtain a low trolley with wheels.
Position: Sunny to semi-shady.
Arrangement: One standard weeping willow (*Salix caprea* "Pendula") with drooping branches that are very attractive. Provide an underplanting of groundcover plants like evergreen periwinkle (*Vinca minor*).

An attractive visual screen
(illustration 5)

Large boxes made of wood are quite suitable for patios as they are usually stable enough to support the weight of a climbing plant espalier. This arrangement can be employed as a windbreak or as a spatial divider.
Container: A box 80 cm

(32 in) wide. The espalier needs plenty of room.
Position: Sunny to semi-shady.
Arrangement: First, plant the climbing plant so that it is slanting toward the espalier that you have already attached to the box. I recommend ivy (*Hedera helix*) or Virginia creeper (*Parthenocissus tricuspidata*).
For the underplanting, choose your favourite dwarf woody plants, small shrubs and perennials. Among these, have at least one species that will grow down over the edge of the vessel.

Arranging several containers

It is usually best to choose uniform colours and materials for containers that will be set close together (see inside front cover and p. 50), particularly if you are intending to combine different shapes such as dishes, large containers and boxes. If all the containers look quite different the effect in such a small space will be a restless jumble. Also ensure that the colours of the flowers do not clash with the flowers in neighbouring containers.

4 *Standards are eye-catching.*

5 *A visual screen.*

Spring-flowering plants in cheerful colours thrive in this box.

A stone trough with three very different species of dwarf spruce.

With or without evergreens

Evergreen deciduous and coniferous shrubs and trees are very popular as they still provide colour even on grey late-autumn days. They are often considered to be easy to care for as they do not lose their leaves or needles in the autumn. This is only partially true, however, as evergreen plants constantly replace old leaves or needles with new ones all year round. They will also lose water through evaporation through their leaves during the winter and are, therefore, particularly at risk of drying out in large containers.

NB: Regularly water the rootstocks of evergreen coniferous and leaf-bearing shrubs and trees throughout the winter, preferably on dull or frost-free days. Avoid wetting the leaves or needles while doing this.

Spring magic
(photograph above)

As early as the second or third month of spring, a balcony box planted with an abundance of woody perennials, dwarf trees, bulbous flowers and biennials will provide a cheerful display of colour.

Container: Wooden box 60 x 20 x 20 cm (24 x 8 x 8 in).
Position and soil: Sunny,

mixture 1 (see p. 11).
Plants used: To the left and right, two Japanese dwarf cherries (*Prunus serrulata*) provide enchanting pink blossom.
Beneath them are red and white tulips (*Tulipa kauffmanniana* hybrids "The First"), lilac and yellow pansies (*Viola cornuta* hybrids), sky-blue forget-me-nots (*Myosotis sylvatica*) and red double daisies (*Bellis perennis*). The daisies will have to be planted anew every year in the autumn. All the other plants should thrive for years in the box, provided they are given adequate care.

A robust planting

(photograph below left)

This heavy stone trough has been planted with evergreen dwarf spruce in graduated shades of green and with different shapes of growth. This kind of arrangement should only ever be kept on a patio because of its weight. The stone vessel has waterproof walls but there are several drainage holes in the base. In order to avoid waterlogging, the trough has been placed on two sections of wooden plank.
Container: Stone vessel 80 x 30 x 30 cm (32 x 12 x 12 in).
Position and soil: Sunny to semi-shady, mixture 1 with added lime (see p. 11).

Plants used: One each of dwarf spruce (*Picea abies* "Aurea", *Picea mariana* "Echniformis" and *Picea orientalis* "Aurea Compacta").

Plants for a sunny balcony

Dry heath landscapes and stony mountain slopes are home to junipers and berberis. If you can cope with their prickly nature, they make ideal plants for a fully sunny balcony. Dwarf juniper and spherical berberis are particularly attractive in their bizarre shapes of growth and they are also evergreen. A creeping heather that will grow over the edge of the trough will help the combination to blend harmoniously.
Container: Box 60 x 20 x 20 cm (24 x 8 x 8 in).
Position and soil: Fully sunny, mixture 1 (p. 11).
Recommended plants: One each of blue dwarf juniper (*Juniperus squamata* "Blue Star"), creeping juniper (*Juniperus communis* "Repanda"), one berberis (*Berberis buxifolia* "Nana").

A delicate effect

In contrast to the bristly needles of pines and junipers, the foliage of *Thuja* and Sawara cypress is soft and delicate. With their

delicate shades of yellow and green, these are true jewels among the evergreen plants. Some varieties will also turn copper during the winter.
Container: A trough with a diameter of 60-80 cm (24-32 in).
Position and soil: Sunny to semi-shady; mixture 1 (p. 11).
Recommended plants: One each of yellow *Thuja occidentalis* "Rheingold", one green dwarf Sawara cypress (*Chamaecyparis pisifera* "Filifera Nana"), one *Microbiota decussata*.

Other attractive evergreen species

Coniferous shrubs and trees:
Lawson cypress (*Chamaecyparis lawsoniana* "Elwoodii"), *Hinoki* cypress (*Chamaecyparis obtusa* "Nana Gracilis"), Chinese juniper (*Juniperus chinensis* "Old Gold"), blue Nepal juniper (*Juniperus squamata* "Blue Carpet"), Norway spruce (*Picea abies* "Echniformis"), Norway spruce (*Picea abies* "Nidiformis"), Canadian spruce (*Picea glauca* "Conica Laurin"), mountain pine (*Pinus mugo pumilio*), blue pine (*Pinus pumila* "Glauca"), Japanese dwarf yew (*Taxus cuspidata* "Nana"), thuja (*Thuja occidentalis* "Danica").
Deciduous shrubs and trees:
Box (*Buxus sempervirens*), dwarf cotoneaster (*Cotoneaster dammeri*), holly (*Ilex crenata*).

Colour all year round

Most people would like to have colourful plants on their balconies and patios all year round. Dwarf shrubs and trees offer colour and interest from late autumn to early spring.

● Orange berries and red autumn foliage are provided by *Euonymus alata*.

● Black berries and green, bizarrely shaped leaves decorate holly (*Ilex crenata*).

● A wealth of yellow flowers are supplied by winter jasmine (*Jasminum nudiflorum*) in late winter.

During the first summer, your neighbours, with their quantities of geraniums and petunias, may be way ahead of you but your permanent planting will make up for this during the following years with its interesting colours and shapes. Have a little patience! Freshly planted young shrubs require a little time to unfold their full splendour.

My tip: A colourful design is usually best in larger areas and can often look oppressive on a small balcony or patio. Here, a design in several shades of the same colour or in a combination of two colours would be more suitable (see pp. 34/35).

Warm autumn colours supplied by a permanent planting in a wooden tub.

Autumn fire

(photograph above)

In the golden autumn light this evergreen plantation with its wealth of red berries will be at its peak. The blue grass (*Festuca cinerea*) provides an interesting contrast to the woody plants.
Container: Tub with a diameter of 80-100 cm (32-40 in).
Position and soil: Semi-shade; mixture 1 (see p. 11).
Plants used: Dwarf cotoneaster (*Cotoneaster dammeri*), dwarf cotoneaster (*Cotoneaster horizontalis*), yellow spindle tree (*Euonymus fortunei* "Emerald'n Gold") and *Festuca cinerea*.

Plants for a shady patio

Even on a relatively shady patio dwarf shrubs and trees will still supply colour all year round.
Container: Tub with a diameter of 80 cm (32 in).
Position and soil: Semi-shady to shady; mixture 2 (p. 11).
Recommended plants: One each of *Corylopsis pauciflora*, heather (*Leucothoe walteri*), hydrangea (*Hydrangea macrophylla*), snowberry (*Symphoricarpos chenaultii*), three evergreen lesser periwinkle plants (*Vinca minor*) and a *Viburnum burkwoodi*.
Planting: The spring-flowering corylopsis and viburnum should be placed in the background. Their wealth of flowers will not be hidden by the late-shooting hydrangea.
The heather, snowberry and periwinkle plants should trail over the edge of the container.

Flowering calendar

This steady progression of flowers begins in the first and second months of spring with the corylopsis and its arresting clusters of yellow flowers and the viburnum with its delicate pink, scented, globular flower umbels. Later, during the second and third months of spring these are followed by the red and white flowers of the heather. The periwinkles unfold their sky-blue flowers in the last month of spring. The pink flowering spikes of snowberry (there are some varieties with white, pink or purple lower umbels) follow in the first and second months of summer. From the first month of autumn onwards, the snowberry will bear red berries. In the autumn, the leaves of the corylopsis will turn golden yellow and will be framed by the fresh green leaves of the periwinkle. The heather is also included among the evergreens but its leaves turn purple red in the winter.
Other recommended species:
Callicarpa bodinieri has lilac pink flowers from the second to third months of summer and pale lilac berries from the first month of autumn. *Fuchsia magellanica* is the hardiest fuchsia. Evergreen: Holly (*Ilex crenata*) bears black-red fruit from the first month of autumn. *Kalmia angustifolia* "Rubra" has dark purple flower umbels from the beginning to the middle of summer. *Mahonia aquifolium* forms forms yellow panicles in the second month of spring.

Summer scents

All of our senses respond to plants. Even if the visual impact of the colours seems to dominate, plants can still be touched, smelled and tasted. This is an easily cared for combination in blue and yellow for people who enjoy scents and spices.
Container: Hanging tub 80 x 30 x 20 cm (32 x 12 x 8 in).
Position and soil: Sunny; mixture 1 (p. 11).
Recommended plants: One *Caryopteris clandonensis*, two *Perovskia atriplicifolia*, two brooms (*Cytisus kewensis*), two *Santolina chamaecyparissus*, one sage (*Salvia officinalis*), one lavender (*Lavandula angustifolia*), four alyssum (*Alyssum saxatile*), three aubreta (*Aubretia hybrids*), two *Sedum reflexum*.
Planting: The *Caryopteris* should be placed in the centre of the tub, the perovskias and brooms near the edges. The other plants should be used to fill up the remaining gaps.

Shrubs and trees with variegated leaves will bring light to your patio even on dull days.

Pieris japonica.

Playing with colours

Deciduous and coniferous colours should be skilfully combined when planting dwarf shrubs and trees. Designs in several shades of one colour are particularly decorative. Choose colours and shades that blend with each other (see p. 26).

My tip: A little white should always be included to enhance the effect of the other colours. Woody plants with variegated leaves can also do this. These plants do not contain chlorophyll in parts of their leaves resulting in yellowish or white, or sometimes red, blue or violet areas if certain pigments are present.

Variegated varieties prefer semi-shade and grow quite slowly so they are well suited to balconies and patios.

Several shades of one colour

(photograph left)

This arrangement of variegated plants would look tranquil and harmonious on any patio.
Containers: A stone trough with a diameter of 40 cm (16 in) and a tub with a diameter of 80 cm (32 in).
Position and soil: Semi-shade; mixture 1 (see p. 11).
Plants used: For the large container or tub, a salmon pink hibiscus (*Hibiscus rosa-sinensis*) and two white variegated *Plectranthus coleoides* "Marginatus". For the small tub an ornamental sage (*Salvia officinalis* "Tricolor").
Unfortunately, all of these plants are sensistive to frost. For a permanent planting in a region with a rough climate, try the following combination instead: one *Weigela florida* "Variegata", with yellow/white-edged leaves and deep pink flowers, two spindle trees (*Euonymus fortunei* "Emerald'n Gold") with golden yellow-edged leaves, one sage (*Salvia officinalis* "Purpurascens") with purple red foliage.

Pastel shades

The pastel hues of violet and its associated shades, from pink through blue, blended with white, are ideal colours for small spaces. In a fully sunny position you can often only really enjoy your balcony in the morning or evening hours during the summer. Delicate colours will conjure up a romantic atmosphere and scented plants like lavender and thyme release a particularly strong perfume at the end of the day. The plants listed below are also very suitable for dry conditions and so are ideal for people who are out at work all day.
Containers: Flowerboxes 60 x 20 x 20 cm (24 x 8 x 8 in).
Position and soil: Sunny; mixture 1 (see p. 11).
Recommended plants: One each of white heather (*Erica carnea*), one cypress (*Chamaecyparis pisifera* "Boulevard"), one lavender (*Lavandula angustifolia*), one pink heather (*Erica carnea*), three pink cushion thyme (*Thymus doerfleri*).
Plant these species at regular intervals in the order listed above, but plant the thyme in front of the others.
Climbers like *Clematis alpina* and *Clematis* hybrids are also suitable for combining, as are many flat-growing shrubs (see p. 27).
For plantings designed in two colours, the best idea is to choose contrasting or complementary colours (see p. 26). Such plantings will produce a cheerful, lively effect without being overcolourful.

Glowing colours

Shady positions demand glowing highlights. Red and white flowers can greatly liven up even very dark and shady patios.
Container: Tub with a diameter of 80 cm (32 in).
Position and soil: Semi-shady to shady; mixture 2 (see p.1).
Recommended plants: One *Pieris japonica* "Flaming Silver", one *Kalmia angustifolia* "Rubra", one holly (*Ilex aquifolium*) as a standard, two rhododendrons, red and white (*Rhododendron* hybrids), two *Skimmia foremannii* and *Skimmia japonica*, four *Cornus canadensis*.
Plant the holly standard in the middle of the container and the broad, bushy growing species around it. The *Cornus* can be used to fill the gaps.

Innovative design

A tree with personality

In the wild, free-standing trees look simply wonderful. Even on balconies and patios, dwarf trees grown in containers (see p. 29) can produce some of the magic of a tree in nature. Plants that like the shade, such as the blue-flowering, evergreen periwinkle (*Vinca minor*), the yellow-flowering nettle (*Lamiastrum galeobdolon*) and the evergreen, yellow-flowering *Epimedium pinnatum colchicum* are suitable as an underplanting.

An ode to autumn
(photograph right)

This rather unconventional evergreen cotoneaster standard is a pleasure to see all year round. With its red berries and an underplanting of asters and autumn crocus (*Colchicum*) (planting time: second/third month of summer), it will provide plenty of colour in the autumn.
Container: Tub with a diameter of 40 cm (16 in).
Position and soil: Sunny; mixture 1 (see p. 11).
Plants used: One cotoneaster standard (*Cotoneaster dammeri*), three pink autumn crocus (*Colchicum hybrids*), four lilac cushion asters (*Aster dumosus*).

The early days of spring
(photograph p. 37)

Fresh green is combined here with the delicate shades of blue and yellow woodland and meadow plants. During the summer the larch will provide bright green colour and then, in autumn, it will turn golden yellow before losing its needles.

Container: A bowl with a diameter of 50 cm (20 in).
Position and soil: Sunny to semi-shady: mixture 1 (see p. 11).
Plants used: One dwarf larch (*Larix kaempferi*), three evergreen periwinkle (*Vinca minor*), seven yellow *Primula acaulis*. Other species that can also be grown as attractive mini trees can be found on page 20.

An unusual autumn combination.

36

Growing your own standards

Many species, such as box (*Buxus sempervirens*), are easy to grow as standards if you follow these simple rules.
● Choose a small, young tree with a very straight stem.
● Regularly remove the lateral shoots from the stem, but not too many in one go as the tree requires sufficient leaves for its metabolic processes.
● Do not cut off the top of the tree until the tree has attained the desired height. This will then stimulate the crown to branch out.
● Continue to remove the tips of the new crown branches until a new bushy crown has formed (this can take up to two years).

Planting a hedge

In an open area, hedges with colourful blooms can be an eyecatching feature at almost any time of year. As they require a lot of room, however, they are generally one of the privileges of owning a large garden. Even on a balcony or patio, however, you can still create the atmosphere of a luxuriant hedge and profit from its many useful qualities. Hedges serve as wind, sun, noise and visual screens. On a large patio you will be able to blend together a colourful company of shrubs in a roomy container. Individual containers with decorative dwarf bushes are recommended for smaller balconies.

Suitable species include the evergreen, blue-leafed berberis (*Berberis verruculosa*), *Callicarpa bodinieri*, evergreen *Pyracantha coccinea* "Orange Glow", *Kerria japonica*, evergreen *Mahonia aquifolium*, as well as viburnum (*Viburnum carlesii*). All of these shade-loving shrubs can be underplanted with suitable low-growing herbaceous perennials.

Delicate needles and colours for the spring.

Innovative design

Miniature landscapes

How lovely it would be to recreate a pretty scene spotted on a walk through nature. Living souvenirs can be much more evocative than any photograph. *But, please, do not dig up any wild plants!* Many species are protected and, anyway, plants taken from the wild will often not grow properly in a garden. It is better to take a good photograph to your garden centre or nursery where you should be able to get plenty of help and advice on putting together a miniature landscape with all the right wild or garden plants. The following examples should give you some ideas to get you started.

Between rocks and moorland
(photograph p. 39)

This small grouping of plants looks really natural growing in a trough made of natural stone.
Container: Granite trough 100 x 40 x 30 cm (40 x 16 x 12 in).
Position and soil: Semi-shade; mixture 1 (see p. 11).
Plants used: One dwarf Weymouth pine (*Pinus strobus* "Minima"), one creeping mountain pine (*Pinus mugo pumilio*), one ivy (*Hedera helix*), one small berberis (*Berberis thunbergii* "Atropupurea Nana"), and one *Stipa capillata*. Interesting colours are provided by two non-hardy plants: the silvery-grey *Senecio bicolor* and a heather (*Erica gracilis*).

Gems by the wayside

If you keep your eyes open while out walking, you are sure to discover some unconventional beauties among the native plants you see. The wild plants used here are particularly robust and grow well, but are often difficult to obtain in the gardening trade so you may need to seek out a specialist nursery.
Container: Tub with a diameter of 40 cm (16 in).
Position and soil: Sunny; mixture 1 (see p. 11).
Recommended plants: One rose (*Rosa villosa*), one broom (*Genista tinctoria*), one broom (*Genista pilosa*) and one *Ononis spinosa*.

Natural magic

Out in the wild, climbing plants scramble over rocks, bushes or trees. They also look very attractive in large containers.
Container: Large tub with a diameter of 40 cm (16 in).
Position and soil: Sunny to semi-shady; mixture 1 (see p. 11).
Recommended plants: One pine (*Pinus mugo* "Mops"), one *Clematis alpina*, one broom (*Genista lydia*).

Plant the pine near the edge of the container. The clematis should be placed near the pine so that it can climb up it. Place the brooms at the foot of the clematis.
NB: Clematis like a lot of sun but need shady roots. In this example, the shade is provided by the broom plants.

Heathland on your doorstep

Heath landscapes have a particular attraction and atmosphere and heather is also evergreen and easy to care for. Provided you choose species and varieties wisely when designing your miniature heathland, you will be rewarded with a planting in which one or other of the plants will always be flowering at any time of the year and in a great variety of different shades.
NB: Individual species have different requirements with respect to soil or compost. The ling (*Calluna vulgaris*), as well as the heather (*Erica tetralix*) and the summer-flowering heather (*Erica vagans*), all require lime-free, acid soils. Only *Erica carnea* will cope with soils containing lime. You will find an example of such a design on page 39.

A small heath landscape has been created in this granite trough.

Winter flowers

Winter jasmine is a most eye-catching plant. Its yellow flowers start to appear in the first month of winter. Plant it with ivy to provide an evergreen framework. Primulas and pansies ensure a display of flowers from early spring onwards.

Container: Hanging container with a diameter of 30 cm (12 in) and a robust chain to suspend it from, along with a stable wall fixture; or a bowl of a similar size that can be set on a pillar.

Position and soil: Sunny; mixture 1 (see p. 11).

Recommended plants: Winter jasmine (*Jasminum nudiflorum*), yellow variegated ivy (*Hedera helix* "Goldheart"). Pansies (*Viola cornuta*) in various colours or primulas (*Primula acaulis*) make a suitable underplanting. Hang or stand this arrangement in an easily visible place in front of a patio or balcony window but in a position sheltered from the wind if possible. During the summer, try to find a semi-shady position for the container. Remember to water it regularly.

Innovative design

A patio all in green and white looks truly elegant.

Cool blue goes well with white.

Beautiful patios

Generally, a patio is the whole family's favourite spot from the middle of spring until the middle of the autumn. During the winter months, the view from your window should be planned to make you look forward to a new round of seasons in your garden. Containers that can be moved about can be placed in different positions according to the season or for decorative effect. For advice on designing with colour and containers please read pages 26-29.

A symphony in white

(photograph above)

The colours green and white dominate on this patio. The

dwarf shrubs and trees in the containers harmonize beautifully with the climbing plants that are growing in open soil.

Box trees (*Buxus sempervirens*) pruned into spherical shapes and grown in containers and ivy (*Hedera helix*) cunningly trained over two wires complete the picture.

Sun and flowers

From early spring until autumn the following plant combination will always provide something new. Even in winter the bare branches of corkscrew hazel will provide an attractive eye-catching feature.

Containers: Two tubs with diameters of 50 cm (20 in) and one of 40 cm (16 in).

Position and soil: Sunny to semi-shady; mixture 1 (p. 11).

Recommended plants: For one large tub *Deutzia gracilis*, *Choenomeles* hybrids, alyssum (*Alyssum saxatile*) and the dwarf *Campanula poscharskyana*. For the second large tub, corkscrew hazel (*Corylus avellana* "Contorta"), *Potentilla fruticosa* "Red Ace", *Aubreta* hybrids and one *Arabis procurrens*.

For the smaller tub, *Euonymus alata*, and *Potentilla fruticosa* "Goldteppich".

A visual screen in warm colours

Plants with yellow or red flowers or leaves seem to trap the sun's rays. Even on dull days, we can still soak up the warmth of these colours. For this example, we chose dwarf shrubs and trees with partly yellow or reddish leaves and warm autumn colours. During the summer, this planting provides a visual screen and is, therefore, particularly suited to form a "wall" dividing the patios of terraced houses.

Container: A box built of stone blocks, 150 cm (60 in) long, 50 cm (20 in) tall and 80 cm (32 in) wide. One ready-made espalier which should be placed in the centre of the box.

Position and soil: Sunny to semi-shady; mixture 1 (see p. 11).

Recommended plants: For the espalier *Parthenocissus quinquefolia* which will climb. If you choose the related species *Parthenocissus tricuspidata*, you can even dispense with an espalier if you stand the container in front of a house wall as this creeper can climb up relatively smooth walls with the help of its adhesive pads. Plant one half of the container with a dwarf plum (*Prunus cistena*) or with *Cotinus coggygria* "Royal Purple", a yellow pillar yew (*Taxus baccata* "Auromarginata"), a purple broom (*Cytisus purpuraeus*), a red cushion

berberis (*Berberis thunbergii* "Atropurpurea Nana"), a yellow *Potentilla fruticosa* "Goldteppich" and a *Potentilla manshurica*.

The second half of the container should be planted with a corkscrew hazel (*Corylus avellana* "Contorta") or a witch hazel (*Hamamelis japonica*) and a broom (*Genista lydia*).

Again add a yellow yew, a red berberis and a potentilla, as described above.

Plant the two tall trees, that is the dwarf plum (*Prunus*) and the corkscrew hazel, slightly off-centre and slightly staggered. The two yews should be placed in the background slightly to both left and right. The brooms and potentillas will hang down over the edge.

Other suitable species include red maple (*Acer palmatum* "Dissectum Atropurpuraeum"), *Euonymus alata, Gaultheria procumbens*, dwarf birch (*Betula nana*) and dwarf weigela (*Weigela florida* "Purpuraea").

Caring for your container shrubs

Life in containers and boxes is not always easy for plants. If you look after your plants properly, however, they will repay your efforts by transforming your balcony or patio for years on end. The following pages will tell you all you need to know about caring for your plants.

Above: The smoke bush displays beautiful colours before its leaves fall.
Left: Autumn on the patio with dwarf shrubs and trees and ripe fruit.

Caring for your container shrubs

Buying plants

Inexperienced gardeners, in particular, should seek advice from a good tree nursery before purchasing any plants. In principle, the following rules apply.

● Using the plant lists (pp. 14/15 and 18/19) choose species and varieties suitable for conditions on your balcony or patio.

● Pick a firm that offers a really good selection of dwarf shrubs and trees.

● The name of the variety and a few brief tips on care should be given on each plant label.

● Choose really young plants as far as possible. They will be more adaptable to a life in pots and containers.

● Choose particularly healthy and robust plants. You will recognize them by a good development of woody parts, stems and branches, vigorous shoots and fresh green leaves or needles, as well as a well-rooted rootstock.

● Check the condition of the plant. It should not have any broken branches, damaged leaves, pests or weeds in its pot.

● Check the growing medium. I do not recommend purchasing plants that have been grown in a pure peat compost. They will usually have originated from mass production and will find it difficult to adapt to new living conditions.

The right way to plant

Spring is the best planting time for dwarf shrubs and trees in containers and flowerboxes. Conifers should be planted before any new shoots appear, if possible, and deciduous trees should not be planted while they are flowering. In both spring and autumn you will be able to obtain woody shrubs and trees with rootstocks wrapped in cloth or sacking. Many tree nurseries also offer container plants cultivated in large containers, which can be transplanted throughout the entire year.

The right way to plant

● Make sure that the container has plenty of drainage holes. Three drainage holes are recommended for a flowerbox with a length of 60 cm (24 in).

● Cover the holes with broken pot shards so that soil cannot be washed out.

● Insert a drainage layer and, if necessary, an insulation layer also (see p. 46).

● Stand dry rootstocks in a bath of water before planting (see p. 47).

● Insert compost (see p. 11) into the container.

● If you are intending to equip a standard with a wooden support post, you should insert it while planting to avoid damaging the roots.

● Compacted rootstocks of container plants can be manually loosened when transplanting.

● Stand the plants in the chosen order in the container and check their height. No plant should end up deeper than it was in its previoius pot, otherwise the lower shoots may begin to decay.

● If the plant is sitting too low down, insert more compost under the roots.

● The cloth around the rootstock need not be removed if it is biodegradable but it should be unknotted.

● The rootstocks of climbing plants should be tilted at an angle towards the support aid; tilt creeping or hanging plants towards the edge of the pot (see illustration 2, p. 46).

● Fill the container with compost to about 2 cm (¾ in) below the edge. Leaving this space will prevent compost from being washed over the edge of the pot when watering.

● Make sure that the gaps between the rootstocks are well filled up with compost.

● If necessary, tie standards to a support stake.

● After planting, press the compost down firmly and water abundantly until water begins to run out of the drainage holes.

● During the next few days, water the plants when they require it but not excessively!

This attractive container is known as a pocket amphora. Plants with fairly small rooting systems can be planted in the pockets. The large opening at the top was planted with an attractive box standard framed by colourful sweet peas. Small pansies grow in all directions out of the pockets.

Drainage, insulation and watering

Good drainage, insulation against the cold and an adequate water supply are all absolutely vital if the plants are to thrive.

Drainage and insulation
(illustrations 1 and 2)

A drainage layer in the bottom of the vessel will prevent waterlogging. Both Hortag and broken pot shards are suitable for this purpose. In small containers and boxes, a depth of 2-5 cm (¾-2 in) will be sufficient; 10 cm (4 in) is recommended for larger containers. You should use Hortag to avoid excessive weight. A fabric insulation layer will prevent compost being washed into the drainage layer. Draw the fabric to the edge of the container (see illustration 1). After planting, any overlapping fabric can be cut off (see illustration 2). Insulating the roots is recommended in regions where heavy frosts and wind can be expected during the winter. Here, a permanent inner insulation layer is shown. (You could also choose to wrap up the outside of the container in late autumn, see p. 51). Thin layers of polystyrene or bubble pack are suitable for this purpose. Line the walls of the container (no gaps) with this material before filling the container with compost.

Watering

The be all and end all of good plant care is watering correctly. You should observe the following basic rules.

● If possible, monitor the humidity of the compost daily with your finger: press a dry forefinger about 1 cm (⅓ in) deep into the compost around the plant. If compost adheres to your finger the medium is still moist and fresh. Dried-out compost will be firm and difficult to press down.

● Water plants that love dry conditions and those that love moist conditions (see tables, pp. 14/15 and 18/19) according to their requirements.

● Never water your plants in intense sunlight. They will be able to absorb water best either in the morning or evening.

● If you have no rainwater handy, you should use water that has been left to stand for a while. Mains water is too cold and will give the plant a shock. It is also usually too full of lime.

● Water vigorously until water is seen to run out of the drainage holes. Superficial watering may result in the lower roots of the plant drying out. The entire surface of the compost should be well soaked.

● If possible, try not to wet the leaves and flowers as this will

1 Drainage and insulation before planting.

2 Drainage and insulation in a container complete with plants.

3 Watering with a wick will free you from watering for a few days.

4 A box with a water reservoir that can supply plants with water for several weeks.

encourage decay and fungal diseases. Also, if the sun is shining, the water droplets will react like magnifying glasses and ugly burn marks will result.

My tip: Cover unplanted compost surfaces with a mulching layer of dried grass cuttings or leaves. This will keep the compost moist longer and delays between watering sessions will be coped with better.

Watering while you are away: Holiday periods can present serious problems for balcony and patio owners with an abundance of plants. Even plants that like dry conditions will not survive several weeks without water during summer temperatures.

The best and simplest solution is always a kind neighbour, friend or relative who will look after your plants. If you wish to try an elaborate, automatically controlled, long-term irrigation system, you should consult an expert at your local garden centre. I would like, however, to introduce you to several simpler possibilities.

Irrigation using a wick
(illustration 3)

The plant pot is standing on a little block just above the surface of the water in a waterfilled container. Depending on the size of the plant pot, one or several wicks (obtainable in the gardening trade), made of absorbent material, lead up through the water drainage holes into the plant pot. (The best plan is to insert these wicks right at the start when you first plant your plants.) The plants are able to soak up water through these wicks during the frost-free seasons of the year. The water reservoir should be sufficient for several days.

Boxes with water reservoirs
(illustration 4)

These special boxes come with a double floor, providing a lower chamber that can be used as a water reservoir. It can be filled from above via a little pipe and the supply will last for about one week. A small window at the bottom of the box allows you to check the water level. The plants are connected with the tank via wicks or strips of fabric which draw up water to meet the needs of the plants.

NB: Please check the information povided by the manufacturer concerning frost-protection.

Full immersion
(illustration 5)

Occasionally, a smaller container may have dried out completely but, even then, complete immersion may still save the plant. Stand the container in a bucketful of water. Hold the container under the surface of the water as long as it takes for bubbles to stop rising to the surface. Then place the container in a position where excess water can run off without causing any damage.

5 Immersing in water: first aid for a plant with a dried out rootstock.

Caring for your container shrubs

Correct fertilizing

A supply of essential nutrients is necessary in order for plants to grow, flower and remain healthy.

● Nitrogen (N) is essential for the growth of leaves and shoots. Well-nourished plants have dark green foliage and grow vigorously. Nitrogen deficiency is signalled by yellowish, small leaves. Too much nitrogen, on the other hand, will make the plants susceptible to disease and lazy to flower.

● Phosphorus (P) stimulates flower formation and the development of fruit. In addition, it encourages the formation of wood. Without phosphorus, there will be few flowers and fruit and the leaves will be yellowish. The plants will become sickly and susceptible to disease.

● Potassium (K) encourages hardiness and is particularly important for permanent plantings. Resistance is also increased. Potassium deficiency is manifested through a yellowish-brown discoloration of the leaf edges.

● Calcium (Ca) is required by plants that thrive on alkaline soil. It is, however, detrimental to plants like rhododendrons which dislike alkaline soils.

● Magnesium (Mg), a constituent of chlorophyll, is particularly essential for evergreen plants. Symptoms of deficiency are yellowish-white, marbled leaves.

In addition to these main nutrients, plants require several elements in small quantities. These are called the trace elements and they will be present in adequate doses in good compost mixtures. Nutrients can be supplied to your plants in various ways.

Controlled-release fertilizers are worked into the compost and only gradually take effect. Among these are hoof and horn chips and blood or bone meal. Potassium and magnesium are, however, not present in adequate quantities in these fertilizers but you will be able to redress the balance by the use of organo-mineral fertilizer mixtures. Potassium, magnesium and trace elements are also contained in wood ash. They are soil-enhancing substances and should be worked superficially into the compost.

A picturesque dwarf maple with spring flowers.

Mineral fertilizers are a preventive against nutrient deficiency during the growth period. Plants that grow vigorously and those with abundant flowers and fruit will require additional doses of fertilizer. You should always cease all fertilizing after the beginning of the autumn so that the wood of dwarf shrubs and trees can ripen properly. There is a huge range of mineral fertilizers for sale in the gardening trade. Always read the dosage instructions on the packaging thoroughly before using them. Overfertilizing should be avoided at all costs.

NB: Freshly planted dwarf shrubs and trees should on no account receive mineral fertilizer as the plants have to root properly first.

Liquid fertilizers are easy to use and are available to the plant immediately. Granulated compound fertilizers that are dissolved in water have the same effect.

Fertilizer sticks were developed specially for balcony plants. They are not recommended for dwarf shrubs and trees, however.

Repotting

Repotting is a measure that prevents nutrient deficiency. If you have small woody plants that are going to grow vigorously, I recommend repotting them annually in spring, following this method.

● Loosen the compost around the edge of the container and take out the plant with its rootstock.

● Shake the old compost out of the rootstock. Very long roots can be shortened and the surface of the rootstock can be roughed up a little. This will stimulate the plant to produce new growth.

● Insert the plant in fresh compost (see planting, p. 44). In later years, when your shrubs and trees have become too large to repot, it is worth partially replacing the compost now and again. For this purpose, mix pure compost with controlled-release fertilizer.

NB: Do try to consider the adverse long-term effects on the environment of using chemical fertilizers and employ them sparingly!

Dwarf cotoneaster.

Caring for your container shrubs

Even in winter this permanent planting will provide something attractive to look at.

Hoar frost on foliage.

Pruning

Many shrubs and trees will stand pruning, while others will not respond well at all (see tables, pp. 14/15 and 18/19). With the exception of yews, dwarf conifers should not be pruned as most species are unable to replace removed branches. Flat-growing junipers that grow beyond the desired size will survive a shortening of the shoot tips.

Planting cut: This is recommended for most flowering bushes and will balance the loss of roots. The branches are cut back by about one third.

Cutting back: Vigorous cutting back will become necessary in the case of many summer-flowering dwarf shrubs and trees. It will encourage an abundance of flowers.

● All species of heather should be cut back to just above the beginning of the shoots after flowering in the spring. Their compact, bushy shape of growth will thus be retained and flowering will be encouraged.

● Sensitive summer-flowering plants that generally freeze back in the winter should be cut back to 10 cm (4 in) above the soil in the spring. They will then form shoots from the base of the roots. The plants will be stronger and bloom better.

● Sub-shrubs, with the exception of *Dryas octopetala*, will cope with considerable cutting back, at which time you can determine the desired height of growth. In the case of evergreen species, for example, lavender, pruning should not be taken back to bare wood.

● Groundcovering deciduous woody plants can be cut back without any problems before they reach the stage of their most luxuriant growth. The shoots will also root easily (see p. 54).

Thinning out cut: *Deutzia*, *Potentilla fruticosa*, lilac, forsythia and spiraea should be thinned out regularly to obtain an abundance of flowers. At intervals of two to three years, the oldest shoots, recognizable by their darker bark and plenty of branching, should be cut out directly above the ground. Take out only a few shoots at a time so that the shape of growth is not spoilt.

Shaping cut: Shrubs and trees that can tolerate pruning, like box, privet, berberis, holly, firethorn and yew, can be shaped properly from the last month of spring to the beginning of summer. Yew and box will even tolerate cutting back into old wood.

● A spherical shape (see photo p. 40): Shape a strong piece of wire into a circle of the desired diameter, which is open at the bottom. Draw it around the plant and push the ends into the compost. Keep turning it around as you cut.

● Cone shape: Stand three bamboo canes in the compost around the plant and tie them up at the top at the desired height of the cone tip. Turn the structure while pruning.

● Spiral (see front cover): Wind a piece of string from the tip evenly downwards in a spiral and tie the end to the stem. If necessary, push a bamboo cane down through the foliage from the tip to hold the tree steady. Then cut out grooves along the course of the string.

Winter protection

All plants in containers and flowerboxes are at risk outside during severe winters as their roots are unprotected by large amounts of soil. In extreme positions, it is a good idea to install an inner layer of insulation around the rootstock (see p. 46). Also stand the container in a position out of the wind, if possible on a wooden pallet. On particularly cold days, you can protect the outside of the containers with layers of bubble pack. The plants themselves should be covered loosely with conifer brushwood. This will protect the shrubs and trees from cold winds and from drying out in winter sunshine.

NB: Evergreen plants should not be covered up too thickly as this would bring the risk of fungus formation.

Mulching: For particularly sensitive species (see table pp. 14/15 and 18/19), I would recommend an additional mulching layer consisting of dried grass cuttings, straw or dry leaves.

NB: Fertilizing too late in late summer or autumn can result in unripe, weakened parts of plants which will then freeze. Winter damage to evergreen plants, for example, brown leaves or brown shoot tips, is generally a sign of damage through dryness. Water evergreen plants regularly on frost-free days.

Pests and diseases

A well-chosen position and expert care are the best and safest plant protection. Weak and uncared-for plants will be susceptible to pests and diseases. In addition, regularly checking plants when watering them will help you to recognize early symptoms of disease and pest infestation. If you act immediately, the plant can usually be saved. This double page spread supplies information on the most important signs of damage and methods of control.

Scale insects

Damage: Sticky leaves, falling leaves. Minute brownish, roundish or comma-shaped scales can be seen on branches and shoots, under which the insects themselves can be seen.
Endangered plants: Box, cotoneaster, juniper, yew.
Remedy: Scratch off the scales and wash off the insects with a 5 per cent soft soap solution. Stand the plants in an isolated position, if at all possible, and observe them carefully for a period of time. Repeat the treatment with soft soap solution after two weeks. A substance based on rape seed oil, which is harmless to useful insects, is available in the gardening trade. This will also work against the tiny, hardly visible larvae.

Mealy bugs

Damage: Crippled growth. Tiny, white, woolly, wax-like tufts can be seen on shoot tips, in particular of pines and spruce. The bugs excrete a sticky fluid which attracts ants.
Endangered plants: Conifers and clematis.
Remedy: As with scale insects, scratch off the woolly coverings and spray with diluted soft soap solution. This treatment should be repeated several times after an infestation.

Spider mites

Damage: Delicate webs, grey-green discoloration and yellow/white specks on the undersides of leaves and shoots. The leaves dry out and drop off. The minute, bright red mites are difficult to see.
Endangered plants: Cotoneaster, broom, ivy, spindle tree, roses, spruce.
Remedy: On sunny days, hose the plants down with a cold, hard stream of water. If the infestation is severe, employ agents containing pyrethrum but make sure they are harmless to bees. High humidity in the air and soil, as well as a good supply of humus, will help to prevent this problem. Overfertilizing, especially with nitrogen, should be avoided.

   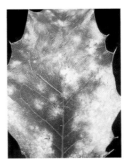

Aphids

Damage: Numerous green or black aphids can be found, particularly on young shoots. The leaves become wrinkled and roll up. The sticky honeydew secreted by the insects is an ideal base for fungal diseases, for example, black spot on roses.
Endangered plants: Roses, ivy and conifers.
Remedy: If infestation does occur, a strong stream of cold water (see spider mites) or a diluted soft soap solution will help. Only if infestation is very severe should pyrethrum-based substances be used, as these will also harm useful insects such as ladybirds and lacewings.

Vine weevil

Damage: Curved pieces eaten out of the edges of leaves can be found on rhododendrons and also on other deciduous trees. The larvae, which resemble cockchafer grubs, eat the bark, shoots and roots near the ground. The plant begins to wilt.
Endangered plants: Rhododendrons and other deciduous trees.
Remedy: The best procedure here is to renew the compost. Shake out the old compost thoroughly and repot the plant with new compost. Avoid a large proportion of peat as these insects love peat-rich soil. With a little luck, you will also be able to collect many of the weevils and their larvae at night during the late spring and early summer.

Rust

Damage: This fungal disease results in tiny black dots or yellow brown pustules appearing all over the undersides of leaves. The uppersides of the leaves display light-coloured spots, then the leaves drop off.
Endangered plants: Broom, heather species, mahonia, roses, willows, elder.
Remedy: Preventive measures are recommended for particularly endangered plants. Mare's tail brew sprayed over the plants and the surface of the compost has yielded good results. The fungus tends to spread more easily in a humid environment, so avoid wetting stalks, stems and leaves when watering, if at all possible.

Powdery mildew

Damage: A white, powdery film on leaves, flowers and young shoots.
Endangered plants: Clematis, heather species, creeping spindle tree, mahonia, *Potentilla fruticosa*, roses.
Remedy: This fungal disease will spread from plant to plant. Preventive measures are particularly important for this problem. Susceptible plants should be regularly sprayed with mare's tail brew or *Polygonum* preparations that are obtainable in the gardening trade. Plants can still be saved using this method even if they are showing the first symptoms of the disease.

Caring for your container shrubs

Propagating dwarf shrubs and trees

Balcony and patio gardeners who like to do a bit of experimenting should also be able to grow some of their own plants. There are two basic ways of propagating:

● generative propagation from seed;

● vegetative propagation from division, rhizomes, layering or cuttings.

Sowing

Sub-shrubs (see table, p. 18) are the easiest plants to sow from seed. They can be started off during the last two months of winter on a warm window ledge and planted outside later on. Other seeds will, however, need pre-treating. The flesh of berries has to be removed and harder shells or skins of seeds have to be "roughened up". This will considerably shorten the germination period. Sow into pots or boxes that can be placed outside. Small seeds should be covered with only a little soil, larger ones with a little more. As soon as the soil begins to warm up in the spring, germination will start. It is important now not to let the soil or compost dry out. Once the plants are strong enough they can be pricked out into individual pots.

Broom (Cytisus species) is an exception. Its seeds should be stored in a cool, dry place after harvesting and not sown out until the following spring. Broom belongs among the light-germinating species and the seed should not be covered with any soil or compost.

NB: Do not forget to make a plan of what you have planted or to label it, as small seedlings are often quite unlike the mature plants they will grow into.

Vegetative propagation

There are various methods of vegetative propagation.

Division is rare among large woody species but usually possible for sub-shrubs. In the spring the entire rootstock can be split up into several parts and replanted. The following are suitable for this method: box, berberis, heather, privet, *Kerria* and snowberry.

Propagation from rhizomes is usually very easy. Many woody species produce new shoots from their roots, which can be cut off. Suitable species for this treatment can be found in the tables on pages 14 and 18.

Layered shoots or cuttings develop from shoots that touch the ground. Many groundcover species produce layered shoots without any help. This method of propagation can be carried out with rhododendron, daphne, lilac and hazel.

Method

● Bend a flexible lateral shoot down to the ground.

● About 20 cm (8 in) from the end of the shoot make a diagonal cut into the shoot.

● The cut can be kept open with the help of a small stone or by wedging a piece of plastic in it.

● Lay the open, cut part in the soil or compost and cover it with a few centimetres of good soil, then weight the whole thing down with a stone.

● Press down the soil or compost and water well. The soil should be kept moist.

Propagation from cuttings is also possible with dwarf shrubs and trees. It does, however, require patience and a little skill. With many species (see tables, pp. 14/15 and 18/19) it will be quite successful.

Method

● During the summer cut off 10 cm (4 in) long shoots.

● Remove all but the top two thirds of the leaves.

● Rooting powder (from the garden trade) will encourage root formation.

● Push the cutting into the soil or compost and water it. A jam jar or transparent foil drawn over the cutting will ensure high humidity. From time to time ventilate it. A warm windowsill is the best position.

● New shoots growing from the cutting indicate that roots have formed. You can now transfer the cutting to a pot.

A pocket amphora with a berry-bearing skimmia and ivy.

Calendar of observation and care

Season	Observations	Watering and fertilizing	Further care	Plant and winter protection
Early to mid spring	**Flowering:** heather, winter hazel, quince, mahonia, daphne. **Shoots:** berberis, birch, *Kerria*.	Carefully water newly shooting woody species. Repot or partially replace with new compost. Work in controlled-release fertilizer.	Cut back summer-flowering bushes. Carry out rejuvenating and thinning out pruning.	Check young shoots and leaves in particular for infestation with pests like aphids; remove winter protection only when no danger of frosts.
Late spring	**Flowering:** broom, rhododendron, hawthorn, snowball, lilac, *Kerria*, *Dryas octopetala*.	Water regularly on warm days, collect rainwater. Work in fresh compost with controlled-release fertilizer or fertilize.	Cut back early flowering woody species like heather and forsythia.	Regularly check for infestation with diseases and pests, treat plants susceptible to mildew with preventive mare's tail extract. Remove winter protection like mulching layers, conifer brushwood and sheeting.
Early to mid summer	**Flowering:** summer lilac, berberis, *Potentilla*, *Kalmia*, St John's wort, spiraea, weigela, roses, rock rose.	Water daily plants in sunny positions on balconies or patios. Additional fertilizer for plants that grow vigorously.	Regularly remove deadheads and wilted leaves.	Continue to check for pests and diseases, also use preventives to control mildew, particularly on roses at this time. Spray with soft soap solution if infestation with aphids occurs.
Late summer to early autumn	**Flowering:** heather, lavender, St John's wort, hydrangea, sage, roses, *Potentilla*, *Caryopteris*. Leaves beginning to turn colour.	Water, depending on the position and the weather. Cease fertilizing so the plant can become hardy.	Remove deadheads and seedstands.	Checking for pests and diseases is particularly important at this time, as plants should be healthy at the start of winter. Mildew is prevalent at the end of summer.

Season	Observations	Watering and fertilizing	Further care	Plant and winter protection
Mid autumn	**Flowering:** heather, fruit, hips on wild roses, dwarf cotoneaster, spindleberry, smoke bush. **Autumn colouring:** sumach, smoke bush. **Yellow:** birch, witch hazel, corkscrew hazel.	Water after leaves have fallen, as the plants hardly lose any water.	Do not carry out any pruning as wounds will not heal well.	Have conifer brushwood and sheeting ready for use as winter protection. Use mulching layer to cover. Stand large containers on grids in a wind-sheltered position.
Late autumn	**Flowering:** heather, roses, *Caryopteris*, roses, skimmia. **Fruit:** hips, snowberries, snowball, privet, yew, cranberry.	Only on a few sunny days, when required. Check moisture content of soil (finger test), water carefully! Keep evergreen plants moist.	Watch weather conditions, only cover containers if frost is severe.	Last check for diseases and pests. Remove fallen leaves of diseased plants.
Early winter	**Flowering:** heather, winter jasmine. **Fruit:** holly, creeping cotoneaster, privet, wild roses, beauty berry.	Water evergreen plants if necessary on frost-free days.		Place winter protection around containers if there is risk of permanent frost. Containers that have inbuilt insulation only need covering.
Mid to late winter	**Flowering:** heather, witch hazel, winter jasmine, corkscrew hazel. **Fruit:** beauty berry, holly, *Catalpa*. **Coloured foliage:** red of mahonia.	Water evergreen plants if necessary on frost-free days.	Protect sensitive woody plants from sun and wind.	Check winter protection. If necessary, remove heavy loads of snow from branches.

Index

Author's notes

This volume deals with the planting and care of dwarf shrubs and trees on balconies and patios and with their propagation. Some of the plants described here are toxic in varying degrees. Lethal plants or even those that are less toxic but might cause health problems in susceptible adults or children have been marked with a ☠ in the tables on pages 14/15 and 18/19. Make absolutely sure that children and domestic pets cannot eat plants or parts of plants that have been marked as dangerous. Also ensure that pots, containers, boxes and hanging containers have been properly and securely fixed. You will find notes on this subject on pages 22/23. Make sure that any additional weight on your balcony through the positioning of furniture and containers does need exceed 250 kg (516 lb) per square metre/yard. If you should suffer an injury while handling soil, consult your physician and get expert advice. Discuss with them the possibility of having a tetanus injection.

All fertilizers and plant protection agents, including organic ones, should be stored in such a way that they are inaccessible to children and domestic pets. Consumption of these substances can lead to severe damage to health. These products should also be kept away from contact with the eyes.

Photographic acknowledgements

Cover photography by L. Rose, Sammer.
Borstell: p. 40 top, 42/43;
de Cuveland: p. 17 bottom right;
Henseler: p. 53 centre left, centre right, right;
Konig: p. 21 centre left;
mein schoner Garten/Krieg: p. 12 right, 16 right, 17 top;
Morell: 43 right; Reinhard: p. 3 left, 13 top, bottom left, bottom right, 17 bottom left, 21 top left, top right, centre right, 34 bottom, 40 bottom,
Sammer: back cover;
Schmidbauer: p. 3 right;
Silvestris/de Cuveland: p. 25 right;
Silvestris/Lochstampfer: p. 13 centre right;
Silvestris/Riedmiller: p. 5 right, 17 centre right, 34 top;
Silvestris/Schwirtz: p. 21 centre, bottom left;
Strauss: front cover, inside front cover, 2, 4/5, 7, 10, 12 left, 16 left, 24/25, 26, 27, 30 top, bottom, 32, 36, 37, 39, 45, 48, 49, 50 top, bottom, 55, 62/63;
Zunke: p. 52 left, centre, right, 53 left.

Cover photographs

Front cover: *Standard Ficus hillii underplanted with Mondo grass, plumbago.*
Inside front cover: *A balcony with box tree pillars.*
Back cover: Containers with autumn arrangements.

Reprinted 1998.

This edition published 1997 by Merehurst Limited
Ferry House, 51-57 Lacy Road, Putney, London SW15 1PR

© 1995 Gräfe und Unzer GmbH, Munich

ISBN 1 85391 685 4

A catalogue record for this book is available from the British Library.

English text copyright © Merehurst Limited 1997
Translated by Astrid Mick
Edited by Lesley Young
Design and typesetting by Paul Cooper Design
Printed in Hong Kong by Wing King Tong

Winter magic on a patio

Even in snow and ice, this balcony presents a charming picture. The green of the evergreen dwarf shrubs and trees and the red colour of the berries are particularly effective under their white covering of snow. Tiny icicles glitter on the bare branches. The many trees and shrubs supply roosting places and shelter for birds which are also able to feed on seeds and grain at the bird table. The snowman with his chestnut eyes and carrot nose provides a centrepiece. Further spots of colour are supplied by the ornamental fowl and globes made of frost-proof ceramic.

A patio need not look sad and bare in the winter. This permanent planting of dwarf shrubs and trees is quite magical when newly covered in fresh snow.